Published by Bradwell Books
9 Orgreave Close Sheffield S13 9NP
Email: books@bradwellbooks.co.uk

Complied by Camilla Zajac

British Library Cataloguing in Publication Data: a catalogue record for this
book is available
from the British Library.

1st Edition
ISBN: 9781902674612

Print: Gomer Press, Llandysul, Ceredigion SA44 4JL
Design by: JenksDesign
Illustrations: ©Tim O'Brien 2013

A Yorkshireman's wife dies and the widower decides that her headstone should have the words 'She were thine' engraved on it.

He calls the stone mason, who assures him that the headstone will be ready a few days after the funeral. Sure enough, the stone mason soon

calls the widower to say that the headstone is ready and would he like to come and have a look.

When the widower gets there he takes one look at the stone to see that it's been engraved 'She were thin'. He explodes – for goodness sake man, you've left the 'e' out - you've left the blooming 'e' out!

The stone mason apologises and assures the poor widower that it will be rectified the following morning. Next day comes and the widower returns to the stone mason - 'There you go sir, I've put the 'e' on the headstone for you'.

The widower looks at the stone and then reads out aloud - 'E, she were thin'.

What can you catch but not throw?

.bloɔ A

The works' boss, young Mr Brown, had to tell old Robert it was time for him to retire after 60 years with the firm.

The old man was indignant:

'So, it's come to this, 'as it? Ah'm not wanted any longer?

Ah worked for thi dad, thi grandad and 'is dad an' all.

Ah tell thi what lad, if Ah'd known this job weren't going to be permanent, Ah'd nivver 'ahe tekken it on'.

A man walks into a bookshop and says 'I hope you don't have a book on reverse psychology.'

I was walking down the street t'other day when ah met me mate.
'Hows tha bin?' He asked.
'I feel like an 'os' ses I
'An 'os?' ses he
'Aye lad, Champion'.

I never was, am always to be.
No one ever saw me, nor ever will.
And yet I am the confidence of all
To live and breathe on this terrestrial ball.
What am I?

Tomorrow.

A photographer up t'hi street advertised that he could retouch photographs.

In walks a woman with a picture of 'er dearly departed husband.

'I'd like this 'eer photo retouched, and while yer at it remove his 'at. I nivver did like that 'at.'

'Aye' said t'photographer chap. 'Now just before you go missus I must know which side he parted his hair.'

'E by gum lad, you must think I am reight daft, you'll find that out when you take his 'at off.'

At a cricket match a fast bowler sent one down and it just clipped the bail.

As nobody yelled 'Ows att' the batsman picked up the bail and replaced it.

He looked at the umpire and said 'Windy today int'it?'

'Ay' said the umpire 'It is. Mind it don't blow thee cap off walking back to t'pavillion'

Harry proudly drove his new convertible into town and parked it on the main street, he was on his way to the recycle centre to get rid of an unwanted gift, a foot spa, which he left on the back seat.

He had walked half way down the street when he realised that he had left the top down... with the foot spa in the back.

He ran all the way back to his car, but it was too late...

Another five foot spas had been dumped in the car.

Did you hear about the two men from the monastery who opened up a seafood restaurant? One was the fish friar, and the other was the chip monk.

A farmer was ploughing his field, looked around and there at the gate was the visiting parson.

So on next his circuit he stopped to pay his respects.

'My, but you and God have built a beautiful place together' said the parson.

'Aye happen you're right, Parson. replied the Farmer, "But between thee 'an me, you should have see it when 'ee had it all to 'issen'.

I have holes in my top and bottom, my left and right and in the middle. What am I?

A sponge.

'Wots up?' asked Joe of one of his colleagues at work.

'It's that there gaffer of ours', says his friend 'He gets right on mi withers.'

'Pay him no heed, do like I do, an' tell him ter get lost.'

A bit later on...

'Well thas a right mate. I did like tha ses and he gave me the sack.'

'Oh, yer not supposed to let him hear yer.'

What did the cheese salesman say?

'That cheese may be Gouda, but this one is Feta!'

Did you hear that they've crossed a Newfoundland and a Basset Hound? The new breed is a Newfound Asset Hound, a dog for financial advisors

What goes round the house and in the house but never touches the house?

The sun.

A couple are playing 'I spy' in the kitchen of their home somewhere in Yorkshire.

'I spy with my little eye something beginning with T' said the husband.

'Tea pot' said the wife. 'Nay Lass!'

'Tea towel?' 'Nay Lass!'

'Toaster?' 'Nay Lass!' he said, drumming his fingers on the work top.

'Oh I don't know' she said at long last 'I give in'

'It's easy' he said. 'It's t'oven!'

From the beginning of eternity
To the end of time and space
To the beginning of every end
And the end of every place.
What am I?

The letter 'e'.

A couple had been courting for nearly twenty years and one day as
they sat on a seat in the park she plucked up courage and asked,
'Don't you think it's time we wed?'
He answered,
'Aye lass, but who'd ave us?'

An Englishman, Irishman and a Scotsman walk into a bar. The Barman says 'Is this a joke?'

A Yorkshire farmer went into a jewellers shop in Harrogate. He was constantly chewing. The salesgirl said, 'Can I help you Sir?'

'Aye' he said, still chewing. 'I'd like one 'o them theer rings'.

'Yes Sir, wedding or engagement?'

'Wedding, tha nos', he said, chewing constantly.

'Gold or Silver?', said the salesgirl, watching him chewing.

'Gold', he said.

'Eighteen Carats?, said the girl.

'Nay lass', he said. 'It's toffee and it's stuck in me teeth'.

How do you know if you're a pirate or not?

You just know you arrrrrhh.

What gear were you in at the moment of the impact?

Gucci sweats and Reeboks.

What does one star say to another star when they meet?

Glad to meteor!

I went into the woods and got it. I sat down to seek it. I brought it home with me because I couldn't find it. What is it?

A splinter.

All about, but cannot be seen.
Can be captured, cannot be held.
No throat, but can be heard.
What is it?

The wind.

When one does not know what it is, then it is something; but when one knows what it is, then it is nothing?

A riddle.

I'm part of the bird that's not in the sky.
I can swim in the ocean and yet remain dry. What am I?

A shadow.

A Yorkshireman was struggling to get home one night, after having had a few drinks when he saw a man from the water board with a big 'T' handle, in the middle of the road opening a valve at the bottom of a manhole.

He walked up behind him and gave him a big shove.

'What's that fer?' said the waterman...

'Thats fer tunin' all t'streets roun' when I'm tryin' ter find mi way home!'

Auld fella walking alongside canal and sees a young lad fair crying his eyes out.

'Wot's tha cryin' fer, young un?'

Through sniffles and bawling, little lad manages to say 'A've loss me mate. Me mate fell in t'canal' and pointed about three feet in front of him.

'By 'eck' says fella and without further ado, strips off his jacket and shoes then jumps into the canal. After few minutes he splashed to side and says, 'Ow old was tha mate?'

By this time, lad had stopped howling and watched the auld fella fair dumbstruck. 'Wot's that mean, 'ow old?'

'Thy mate" said fella, 'Ow old were 'e? Wor 'e a big lad?'

Little lad scowled at the old man, 'Nah! Tha daft bat. Not me mate - me mate outa me saniches'

Two old ladies talking in a Dales village, one says to the other, 'You can tell t' winter's cummin cos t'butter's 'ard '.

An old Yorkshireman and a well spoken educated businessman were sat in a pub talking about a local lad who had grown up and made a good life for himself.

The Yorkshireman says, 'Ah knew yon lad fri bein a nipper an gerrin rahnd baht britches an nah booits to 'is feet.'

The businessman says, 'That may be, but I can remember him playing out wearing neither trousers nor shoes.

A Yorkshireman's Grace

God bless us all, an' mak us able
Ta eyt all t' stuff 'at's on this table...

To follow an ungenerous meal:
We thank the Lord for what we've getten:
Bud if mooare 'ad been cutten
Ther'd mooare 'a' been etten...

Why is 6 afraid of 7?

Because 7, 8, 9!

Tha can allus tel a Yorkshireman, but tha can't tell him much...

Two snowmen are standing in a field. One says to the other 'That's funny, I can really smell carrots.'

The Yorkshire Coat of Arms
A Flea, A Fly, A Magpie, an' Bacon Flitch
Ist' Yorkshermans Coit of Arms
And t'reason they've chozzen these things so rich
Is becoss they hav'all speshal charms.
A Flea will bite whoivver it can-- An soa, my lads, will a Yorksherman!
A Fly will sup with Dick, Tom or Dan An' soa, by gow! will a Yorksherman!
A Magpie can talk for a terrible span - An' soa an all, can a Yorksherman.
A Flitch is no gooid whol its hung, ye'll agree No more is a Yorksherman, don't ye see.

What is the longest word in the English language?
Smiles. Because there is a mile between its first and last letters.

What do you do if you are driving your car in central London and you see a space man?
Park in it, of course.

A Yorkshire vet had finished for the day and to check there was no-one waiting shouted from his surgery into the waiting room

'Is there anyone left in there?'

A man replied 'Only me, vet'

Vet asks 'What is is?'

'Cat's reet poorly' came the reply.

Vet asks 'Is it a Tom?

'No, I brought it wi' me'

What do you call a pie on top of
Barnsley town hall clock?
Something ta eight.

Why do seagulls live by the sea?

Because if they lived by the bay they would be called bagels.

Why was the scarecrow promoted?

He was outstanding in his field!

What's brown and sticky?

A twig.

At an antiques auction in Leeds, a wealthy American announced that he had lost his wallet containing £5,000, and he would give a reward of £50 to the person who found it. From the back of the hall a Yorkshire voice shouted, 'I'll give £100!'

Did you hear about the man who was convicted of stealing luggage from the airport?
He asked for twenty other cases to be taken into account.

They say an Englishman laughs three times at a joke. The first time when everybody gets it, the second a week later when he thinks he gets it, the third time a month later when somebody explains it to him.

Stan and Alf are two Yorkshiremen working at the local sawmill. Alf is very accident prone. One day Alf slips and his arm gets caught and severed by the saw. Stan quickly puts the arm in a plastic bag and rushes it and Alf to the local hospital. Next day, Stan goes to the hospital and asks about Alf. The nurse says, 'Oh he's fine, we've reattached his arm'. The very next day he's back at work in the saw mill.

Within a couple of days Alf has another accident and severs his head. Stan puts the head in a plastic bag and transports it and Alf to the hospital. Next day he goes in and asks the nurse how Alf is. The nurse breaks down and cries and says, 'He's dead'. Stan is shocked, but not surprised, and says to the nurse: 'I suppose the saw finally did him in'.

'No', says the nurse, 'Some idiot put his head in a plastic bag and he suffocated'.

What comes once in a minute, twice in a moment, but never in a thousand years?

The letter M.

What goes around the world but stays in a corner?

A stamp.

A kid from Yorkshire starts school and his dad gives him two pounds for the bus home. Instead of getting on the bus the kids runs behind it all the way home. Dad comes home from the pub and the kid says, 'Dad I saved you two quid today because I ran behind the bus instead of getting on'.

The dad sends him to bed without supper saying, 'You should have run behind a taxi and saved me 40 quid you little...'

A group of chess enthusiasts checked into a hotel and were standing in the lobby discussing their recent tournament victories. After about an hour, the manager came out of the office and asked them to move. 'But why?' they asked, as they walked off. 'Because,' he said 'I can't stand chess nuts boasting in an open foyer.'

A Yorkshire man had emigrated to America, but still used to receive news from home by mail.

One day, he received the following telegram:

'Regret father died this morning STOP

Early hours. Funeral Wednesday STOP

Yorkshire two hundred and one for six STOP

Boycott not out ninety six.'

Four old retired gentlemen are walking down a street in London. They turn a corner and see a sign that says, "Old Timers Bar - All drinks 10p." They look at each other and then go in, thinking, this is too good to be true.

Graeme, the old bartender says in a voice that carries across the room, 'Come on in and let me pour one for you! What'll it be, gentlemen?'

Each man orders a Martini. In no time the bartender serves up four Martinis and says, 'That'll be 10p each, please.'

The four men stare at the bartender for a moment, then at each other. They can't believe their good luck. They pay the 40p, finish their Martinis, and order another round.

Again, four Martinis are produced, with the bartender again saying, 'That's 40p, please.' They pay the 40p, but their curiosity gets the better of them. They've each had two Martinis and haven't even spent a £1 yet. Finally one of them says, 'How can you afford to serve Martinis as good as these for a 10p a piece?'

'I'm a retired tailor,' the bartender says, 'and I always wanted to own a bar. Last year I won £25 million in the lottery and decided to open this place. Every drink costs 10p. wine, beer, whatever.'

'Wow! That's fantastic!' one of the men says.

As the four of them sip at their Martinis, they can't help noticing seven other people at the end of the bar who don't have any drinks in front of them and haven't ordered anything the whole time they've been there. Nodding at the seven at the end of the bar, one of the men asks the bartender, 'What's with them?'.

The bartender says, 'They're retired people from Yorkshire. They're waiting for Happy Hour when drinks are half-price.'

What do you give a sick budgie?
Tweetment.

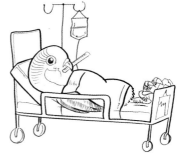

Me and the wife walked past a posh
new restaurant last night...
... 'Did you smell that food?"'she
asked... 'Wonderful!'
Being the kind hearted generous Yorkshireman
that I am, I thought,
'What the heck, I'll treat her!
So we walked past it again.

A London lawyer and a Yorkshireman are sitting next to each other on a long flight to Leeds.

The lawyer is thinking that Yorkshiremen are all 'cloth cap and clogs' and that he can fool them easily...

So the lawyer asks if the Yorkshireman would like to play a fun game.

The Yorkshireman is tired and just wants to take a nap. He politely declines and tries to catch a few winks. The lawyer persists and says that the game is a lot of fun.

'I ask you a question, and if you don't know the answer, you pay me only £5; you ask me one, and if I don't know the answer, I will pay you £500.' This catches the Yorkshireman's attention and he agrees to play the game.

The lawyer asks the first question. 'What's the distance from the Earth to the moon?'

The Yorkshireman doesn't say a word, reaches in his pocket, pulls out a five-pound note, and hands it to the lawyer.

Now, it's the Yorkshireman's turn. He asks the lawyer, 'What goes up a hill with three legs, and comes down with four?'

The lawyer uses his laptop, searches all the references he knows. He uses the air-phone; he searches the web and even the British Library. He sends e-mails to all the clever friends he knows, all to no avail. After over an hour of searching, he finally gives up.

He wakes up the Yorkshireman and hands him £500. The Yorkshireman pockets the £500 and goes straight back to sleep.

The lawyer is going crazy not knowing the answer. He wakes the Yorkshireman up and asks, 'Well! What goes up a hill with three legs and comes down with four?'

The Yorkshireman reaches in his pocket, hands the lawyer £5 and goes back to sleep.

What do you call a Yorkshireman who refuses a free drink on his birthday?
Dead!

What walks all day on its head?

A nail in a horse shoe.

Why should you never ask a person if they come from Yorkshire?
Because if they are not from Yorkshire, they'll be insulted. And if they are from Yorkshire, they'd have told you already.

What is it that you can keep after giving it to someone else?

Footsteps.

I met a man in Yorkshire the other day. I knew he was dyslexic as soon as I saw him. He had a cat flap on his head.

The more you take, the more you leave behind. What are they?

Your word

A Yorkshire farmer was visited by a Texan farmer....

Texan. 'How big is your farm?'

Tyke. 'See them trees yonder? that's the boundary of my farmland'

Texan. 'Heck, it takes me three days to drive to the boundary of my farm'

Tyke. 'I had a car like that once'

Though it is not an ox, it has horns; though it is not an ass, it has a pack-saddle; and wherever it goes it leaves silver behind. What is it?

A snail.

"Brothers and sisters have I none, yet that man's father is my father's son" who is "that man"?

That man is your son.

A box without hinges, key, or lid, yet golden treasure inside is hid. What is it?

An egg.

A man enters a dark cabin. He has just one match with him. There is an oil lamp, a wood stove, and a fireplace in the cabin. What would he light first?

The match.

What is it that never asks you any questions and yet you answer?

Your phone.

My life can be measured in hours;
I serve by being devoured.
Thin, I am quick; fat, I am slow.
Wind is my foe.
What am I?

A candle.

I give you a group of three. One is sitting down and will never get up. The second eats as much as is given to him, yet is always hungry. The third goes away and never returns. What are they?

A stove, fire and smoke.

Your mother's brother's only brother-in-law is your Stepfather, Grandfather, Uncle or Father?

Your Father.

Six dozen dozen is greater than half a dozen dozen   yes or no?

No, both are equal.

A Leeds man walks into a High Street bank and asks for a loan.

He tells the bank manager he is going to Australia on business for two weeks and needs to borrow £5,000.

The bank manager tells him that the bank will need some form of security for the loan, so the Yorkshire lad hands over the keys and documents of a new Ferrari parked on the street in front of the bank. He produces the log book and everything checks out.

The bank manager agrees to accept the car as collateral for the loan.

The bank manager and his officers are bemused by the casually dressed Yorkshireman using a £120,000 Ferrari as collateral against a £5000 loan.

The bank manager then instructs an employee of the bank to drive the Ferrari into the bank's underground garage, where he parks it.

Two weeks later, the man returns, repays the £5,000 and the interest of £15.41.

The bank officer says to the Yorkshireman, 'Sir, we are very happy to have had your business and this transaction has worked out very nicely, but we are a little puzzled.

While you were away, we checked you out further and found that you are a multi-millionaire.

What puzzles us is, why would you bother to borrow £5,000?'
The Yorkshireman replies: 'Where else in Leeds can I park my car for two weeks for only £15.41 and expect it to be there when I return?'

You can have me but cannot hold me;
Gain me and quickly lose me.
If treated with care I can be great,
And if betrayed I will break.
What am I?

Trust.

When I am filled,
I can point the way;
When I am empty,
Nothing moves me.
I have two skins.
One without and one within.
What am I?

A glove.

My thunder comes before the lightning;
My lightning comes before the clouds;
My rain dries all the land it touches.
What am I?

A volcano.

What kind of coat can only be put on when wet?

A coat of paint.

What jumps when it walks and sits when it stands?

A kangaroo.

Four men sat down to play.
and played all night till break of day.
They played for gold and not for fun.
with separate scores for every one.
Yet when they came to square accounts.
they all had made quite fair amounts!
Can you the paradox explain?
If no one lost. how could all gain?

The four men were all fiddlers in a band and were each paid £5
at the end of the night. It is tempting to assume that they were
playing cards. but that is not stated!

Why couldn't Cinderella be a good soccer player?
She lost her shoe, she ran away from the ball, and her coach was a pumpkin.

What do you call a boomerang that won't come back?

A stick.

Two aerials meet on a roof - fall in love - get married. The ceremony was rubbish - but the reception was brilliant.

Did you know that Yorkshire is mentioned in the Bible? Apparently three wise men came from the East Riding on camels.

What do you call a hippie's wife?

Missssippi.

Two boys were arguing when the teacher entered the room.
The teacher says, 'Why are you arguing?'
One boy answers, 'We found a ten pound note and decided to give it to whoever tells the biggest lie.
'You should be ashamed of yourselves,' said the teacher, 'When I was your age I didn't even know what a lie was.'
The boys gave the ten pound note to the teacher.

I am seen in places that appear to need me not.
I come seldom to places that need me most.
Sometimes my arrival is celebrated.
at others times I am hated.
I refresh all things whether they need it or not.

Rain.

If vegetarians eat vegetables, what do humanitarians eat?

What. when you need it you throw it away. but when you don't
need it you take it back?

An anchor.

Who succeeded the first Prime Minister?

The second one!

What did Geronimo shout when he jumped out of the aeroplane?

ME!

A man wanted to become a monk so he went to the monastery and talked to the head monk.

The head monk said, 'You must take a vow of silence and can only say two words every three years.'

The man agreed and after the first three years, the head monk came to him and said, 'What are your two words?'

'Food cold!' the man replied.

Three more years went by and the head monk came to him and said 'What are your two words?'

'Robe dirty!' the man exclaimed.

Three more years went by and the head monk came to him and said, 'What are your two words?'

'I quit!' said the man.

'Well', the head monk replied, 'I'm not surprised. You've done nothing but complain ever since you got here!'

A duck walks into a pub and goes up to the barman.

The barman says 'What can I get you?'

Duck: 'Umm. Do you have any grapes?'

Barman (Looking surprised):

'No, I'm afraid we don't.'

The duck waddles slowly out of the pub.

The next day at the same time, the duck waddles into the pub, hops up on a bar stool.

Barman: 'Hi. What can I get for you?'

Duck: 'Um. Do you have any grapes?'

Barman (a little annoyed): 'Hey! Weren't you in here yesterday. Look mate, we don't have any grapes. OK?'

The duck hops off the stool and waddles out of the door.

The next day, at the same time, the barman is cleaning some glasses when he hears a familiar voice

Duck: 'Umm.. Do you have any grapes?'

The barman is really annoyed

Barman: 'Look. What's your problem? You came in here yesterday asking for grapes, I told you, we don't have any grapes! Next time I see your little ducktail waddle in here I'm going to nail those little webbed feet of yours to the floor. GOT me pal?'

So the duck hops off the bar stool and waddles out.

The next day at the same time, the duck waddles into the pub, walks up to the barman and the barman says,

'What on earth do YOU want?'

'Errrr. do you have any nails?'

'What!? Of course not.'

'Oh. Well, do you have any grapes?'

What do you get when you cross a dog with a telephone?

A Golden Receiver!

What do cats like to eat for breakfast?

Mice Krispies

A new client had just come in to see a famous lawyer.

'Can you tell me how much you charge?', said the client.

'Of course', the lawyer replied, 'I charge £200 to answer three questions!'

'Well that's a bit steep, isn't it?'

'Yes it is,' said the lawyer, 'And what's your third question?'

A Yorkshire man had emigrated to America, but still used to receive news from home by mail.

One day, he received the following telegram:

'Regret father died this morning STOP

Early hours. Funeral Wednesday STOP

Yorkshire two hundred and one for six STOP

Boycott not out ninety six.'

I am so small, and sometimes I'm missed.
I get misplaced, misused, and help you when you list.
People usually pause when they see me.
So can you tell me what I could be?

A comma.

Light as a feather,
Nothing in it.
Few can hold it.
For even a minute.

Your breath.

Language student to teacher, 'Are 'trousers' singular or plural?'
Teacher, 'They're singular on top and plural on the bottom.'

A customer ordered some coffee in a café. The waitress arrived with the coffee and placed it on the table. After a few moments, the customer called for the waitress 'Waitress,' he said, 'There's dirt in my coffee!', 'That's not surprising, sir', replied the waitress, 'It was ground only half an hour ago.'

What kind of ears does an engine have?
Engineers

A passenger in a taxi tapped the driver on the shoulder to ask him something.

The driver screamed, lost control of the cab, nearly hit a bus, drove up over the curb and stopped just inches from a large plate glass window. For a few moments everything was silent in the cab, then the driver said, 'Please, don't ever do that again. You scared the daylights out of me.'

The passenger, who was also frightened, apologised and said he didn't realize that a tap on the shoulder could frighten him so much, to which the driver replied, 'I'm sorry, it's really not your fault at all. Today is my first day driving a cab. I've been driving a hearse for the last 25 years.'

What lies at the bottom of the ocean and twitches?

A nervous wreck.

How many Yorkshire men does it take to change a lightbulb?
What does tha' mean? Its a perfectly good blooming lightbulb and has worked for thousands of years.

A man walks into a doctor's office with two onions under his arms, a potato in his ear and a carrot up his nose. He asks the doctor: 'What's wrong with me?'
The doctor replies: 'You're not eating properly.'

Where do generals keep their armies?

Up their sleevies.

The leader of a leading vegetarian society just couldn't control himself any more. He just needed to try some pork, just to see what it tasted like. So one summer day he told his members he was going away for a break. He left town and headed to the nearest restaurant. After sitting down, he ordered a roasted pig, and impatiently waited for his delicacy. After just a few minutes, he heard someone call his name, and to his horror he saw one of his fellow members walking towards him. Just at that same moment, the waiter walked over, with a huge platter, holding a full roasted pig with an apple in its mouth. 'Isn't that something,' says the man after only a moment's pause, 'All I do is order an apple, and look what it comes with!

What's the difference between roast beef and pea soup?

Anyone can roast beef.

A man drives past a country pub on the outskirts of Barnsley and decides to go back in for a swift half. As he approaches the front door he sees four old men sitting on a bench wearing flat caps. 'Afternoon lads' says the bloke. The old men just mumbled something under their breaths in reply, so he went into the bar and ordered a pint. '1p says the barman. '1p, how come it's so cheap?' asks the punter. 'It's the 100th anniversary of the pub today and I'm celebrating by selling beer at the price it would have been when it opened' replies the barman. 'Great, but if you don't mind me asking, What's wrong with those lot on the bench?' says the guy. "Take no notice mate, they're upset 'cos I'm not having a happy hour'

What time does Sean Connery arrive at Wimbledon?

Tennish.

What always ends everything?

The letter 'g'.

A man went on a trip on Friday, stayed for two days and returned on Friday. How is that possible?

Friday is a horse!

What five letter word can have its last four letters removed and still sound the same?

QUEUE - remove "UEUE", say Q. Q and queue are pronounced the same.

When is a yellow dog most likely to enter a house?

When the door is open.

A man is rushing to a hospital from a business trip because his wife has just gone into labour with twins, and there is a family tradition that the first family member to arrive gets to name the children. The man is afraid his wayward brother will show up first and give his kids horrible names. When he finally arrives at the hospital in a cold sweat he sees his brother sitting in the waiting room, waving, with a silly grin on his face. He walks unhappily in to see his wife who is scowling and holding two little babies, a boy and a girl. Almost afraid to hear it, the man asks, 'What did he name the girl?' 'Denise' says the wife. 'Hey that's not too bad! What did he name the boy?' 'De-nephew.'

The old king is dying, and wants to leave his kingdom to the wiser of his two sons. He tells them that he will hold a horse-race, and the son whose horse is the last to reach the bridge and come back will inherit the realm. Immediately the younger son jumps on a horse and makes for the bridge at top speed. The king now knows that this is the wiser son, and leaves him the kingdom. Why?

The younger son jumped on the older son's horse. He realized that if they rode their own horses the race would never end.

How many cats are in a small room if in each of the four corners a cat is sitting, and opposite each cat there sit three cats, and at each cat's tail a cat is sitting?

Four cats - each near the tail of the cat in the adjacent corner (it's a small room!)

I do not breathe, but I run and jump.
I do not eat, but I swim and stretch.
I do not drink, but I sleep and stand.
I do not think, but I grow and play.
I do not see, but you see me every day.

I am a leg.

A girl who was just learning to drive went down a one-way street in the wrong direction, but didn't break the law. How come?

She was walking.

If it's not the day after Monday or the day before Thursday, and it isn't Sunday tomorrow, and it wasn't Sunday yesterday, and the day after tomorrow isn't Saturday, and the day before yesterday wasn't Wednesday, what day is it?

Sunday.

A Yorkshire aerobics instructor said to his class "Hands on thighs" so they all did. None of them could see a thing.

Unusual Yorkshire place names:
Slack Bottom, near Hebden Bridge
Ainderby Quernhow, near Thirsk, North Yorkshire.
Blubberhouses, near Menwith Hill, North Yorkshire
Booze, Arkengarthdale, North Yorkshire
Kirkby Overblow, south of Harrogate, North Yorkshire
Mankinholes, near Todmorden, West Yorkshire
Wigglesworth, North Yorkshire
Yockenthwaite, in Wharfedale, North Yorkshire.

It was late in the day and the two Yorkshire Puddings had been out skiing and then gone on to have rather too much to drink. As they tried to ski away from the panorama at the top of the mountains, they started having a heated argument about what they were looking at in the heavens.

One said the big round thing they could see was the sun, whilst the other was equally certain it was the moon.

Seeing the only other skier still on the slopes they appealed to him for help, and the second Yorkshire Pudding yelled out 'Ah Say, mister, isn't that the sun?'

The first Yorkshire Pudding wanted his say 'Nay, it's t'moon, isn't it?'

The lone skier (also a Yorkshireman) didn't want to get involved and replied 'Well, to tell ye the truth, Ah'm a stranger in these parts!'

A depressed-looking man is sitting in a cheap, greasy diner in a Leeds suburb. He picks up the menu and sees that it contains just three dishes: meatloaf, shepherd's pie and Yorkshire pudding. The waitress comes over to take his order. 'I'll have the Yorkshire pudding,' says the man glumly, 'And if you could throw in a few kind words that would be very welcome.' The waitress leaves and returns a few minutes later with a plate of Yorkshire pudding. She bangs the plate on the table in front of the man and starts to walk off. 'Hey,' says the man. 'I got my dinner; how about those kind words?' The waitress turns, takes the cigarette out her mouth and says, 'Don't eat the pudding.'

Who is the roundest knight at King Arthur's table?

Sir Cumfrence

Joshua loved to go to his local for a pint. Unfortunately the new landlord did not allow dogs, and Joshua had a whippet – Ben - the best whippet in all Yorkshire.

So that night, when Joshua entered the pub. the landlord came over.

'No dogs allowed, Josh,' he said. 'It's the rules.'

'Aye,' whined Josh, 'But it's only my whippet, Ben.'

'I know', said the landlord, 'But he's a dog and he's not allowed.'

Josh trudged out of the door, dejected. But just outside he met old, blind Abraham.

'Hello Josh,' said Abraham. 'Coming for a pint?'

'I can't,' sighed Josh. 'No dogs allowed.'

'Why, that's nonsense,' cried Abraham. 'You leave it to me!.'

So they walked into the pub, and the landlord rushed over and said,

'I told you - no dogs allowed!'

'But he's my new guide-dog,' said Abraham, 'You must allow guide-dogs, surely?'

'Guide dog?' scoffed the landlord. Everyone knows that guide-dogs are always Labradors or golden retrievers or such like.' Abraham cocked his head to one side. 'Oh aye,' he said, 'So what did they give me?'

How many whippets can you fit in a queen-size bed?

NONE..... the queen has Corgis!

What has five eyes, but cannot see?

The Mississippi River.

A Yorkshireman says to his wife, 'Get your coat on luv, I'm off to the club'.
His wife says, 'That's nice you haven't taken me out for years'.
He says, 'You're not coming with me, I'm turning the heating off when I go out'.

A man builds a house rectangular in shape. All the sides have southern exposure. A big bear walks by. What colour is the bear? Why?

The bear is white because the house is built on the North Pole.

What type of cheese is made backwards?

Edam.

What starts with a 'P', ends with an 'E' and has thousands of letters?

The Post Office!

Popular Yorkshire sayings

See all, 'ear all, say nowt. Eat all, sup all, pay nowt. An' if th'ivver does owt for nowt, allus do it for thissen

Ee, by gum

Tha' can allus tell a Yorkshireman, but tha' can't tell 'im much

Well, Ah'll go to t'foot of ahr stairs

It's neither nowt nor summat

Put t'wood in t'ol

Wheere ther's muck, ther's brass

'Ey up

An' Ah'll tell thi that fer nowt

Why won't a witch wear a flat cap?
Because there's no point in it.

I've just bought some of that L'Oreal Yorkshire shampoo.
It's made with Eyup Vera.
Cos tha's worth it.

In Yorkshire, a woman and her husband heard a man driving down the road shouting 'The world is ending!'.

The wife said 'Don't worry. It's only Farmer Geddon!'

Why did the whippet cross the road?
Because some bunny was over there!

How do you make a Yorkshire omelette?
First nick three eggs...

What do you get if you cross a nun and a chicken?

A pecking order!

Man in deepest Yorkshire calls his son in Devon the day before Christmas Eve and says, 'I hate to ruin your day but I have to tell you that your mother and I are divorcing; forty-five years of misery is enough.'

'Dad, what are you talking about?' the son screams.

'We can't stand the sight of each other any longer' the father says. 'We're sick of each other and I'm sick of talking about this, so you call your sister in Bristol and tell her.'

Frantic, the son calls his sister, who explodes on the phone. 'Like hell they're getting divorced!' she shouts, 'I'll take care of this!'
She calls Yorkshire immediately, and screams at her father 'You are NOT getting divorced. Don't do a single thing until I get there. I'm calling my brother back, and we'll both be there tomorrow. Until then, don't do a thing, DO YOU HEAR ME?'' and hangs up.

The old man hangs up his phone and turns to his wife. 'Sorted! They're coming for Christmas - and they're paying their own way.'